AF271765

FEMINISM IN CHRISTIANITY

Contemporary Life Series

Book 5

Feminism in Christianity

AN ORTHODOX
CHRISTIAN RESPONSE

Second Edition

DEBORAH (MALACKY) BELONICK

ST VLADIMIR'S SEMINARY PRESS
YONKERS, NEW YORK
2012

Orthodox Church in America (OCA)

Library of Congress Cataloging-in-Publication Data

Belonick, Deborah.
  Feminism in Christianity : an Orthodox Christian response / by Deborah
Malacky Belonick.
      p. cm.
  Originally published: Syosset, N.Y. : Dept. of Religious Education, Orthodox
Church in America, 1983.
  Revision of the author's thesis (master's)—St. Vladimir's Orthodox
Theological Seminary. Includes bibliographical references (p.)
      ISBN 978-0-86642-045-7
      1. Feminism—Religious aspects—Orthodox Eastern Church. 2. Women in
the Orthodox Eastern Church. 3. Orthodox Eastern Church—Doctrines.
I. Title.

  BX342.5.B45 2012
  281.9082—dc23

                                                            2011028426

ISBN 978-86642-045-7

Orthodox Christian Publications Center works are now published by

ST VLADIMIR'S SEMINARY PRESS
575 Scarsdale Road, Yonkers, NY 10707
1-800-204-2665
www.svspress.com

PRINTED IN THE UNITED STATES OF AMERICA

Contents

Preface

This little book first was published in 1983, a good twenty years after the Women's Movement had been launched on U.S. soil. It appeared as an abbreviated version of my Master of Divinity thesis,[1] and its purpose was twofold: to investigate the ripple effects the waves of feminist thought had produced in religious communities, and to determine whether or not the backwash was congruent with my own Orthodox Christian faith.

I did, and it was not.

At the time it was first written, I intended the work to be a clarion call for Orthodox Christians. In my mind, ripples of feminist thought were already turning into tidal waves that quickly were erasing major areas of beachhead once recognizably marked as traditionally Christian: an unchangeable canon of Holy Scripture; a male Jesus, risen bodily from the dead; a Trinity with the names "Father, Son, and Holy Spirit"; and a General Resurrection where men would remain male and women would remain female.

The content in this newly published edition has not changed. The volume remains a comparison between feminist theology and Orthodox Christian theology, casting the distinctions between the two in sharp relief. I have purposefully *not* changed my '80s thoughts, mostly because I still believe in my conclusions, and partly

[1] Editor's Note: Deborah (Malacky) Belonick was the 1979 valedictorian of her class at St Vladimir's Orthodox Theological Seminary, Yonkers, NY. Her Master of Divinity thesis was originally titled: *The Spirit of the Female Priesthood;* it is unpublished and held at St Vladimir's Seminary Library. She wrote the thesis to explore the particular feminist theology that had supported the ordination of the first eleven women to be ordained in the Episcopal Church, USA, in 1974. Since writing her thesis, she has remained an outspoken opponent of women's ordination to the priesthood in the Orthodox Christian Church.

for fear of removing the original argumentation from its 20th-century context.

What has changed is the style; I have streamlined sentences to read less like a truncated master's thesis and more like a primer. I've also corrected some footnotes.

The only 21st-century editions I have made, for clarity, lie in the definition of two words: the word "sex" in this volume now refers to biological and physical characteristics (female and male); while "gender" refers to behaviors, attributes, and modes of personal expression (feminine and masculine), whether socially constructed or innately programmed into human beings—depending on what you believe, and I still believe the latter.

All of which is not to say that my thoughts have not progressed since writing this book, or that my research has not been refined. Indeed, since this book was published, I have plunked bits and pieces of research into many file folders with labels such as: Gender, Headship, Deaconesses, Marriage, Celibacy, Household of Faith, Menstruation, Head Coverings, Women's Silence, Genetic/Neuro-Studies, and Image of God. Using this research, I have published several smaller articles in theological and popular journals and have contributed to a few books dealing generally with "women in the church."[2]

At the time that I wrote my master's thesis, I wish that I would have had access to some of my subsequent research, which would have further illumined and supported—but not contradicted—the arguments set forth in the original text. Some of this research further refutes feminist theology, while other research clarifies some long-held (but erroneous) views of women and their ministry within the Orthodox Christian context.

I wish that I had had in hand, for example, *Letter XLVIII to Amun*, from Athanasius, Archbishop of Alexandria, and St Gregory the Great's Letter to St Augustine. Both seem to support a woman's

---

[2]Most notably, "Testing the Spirits," in *Women and the Priesthood*, ed. Thomas Hopko, (Crestwood, NY: St Vladimir's Seminary Press), pp. 189–223.

prerogative to receive Holy Communion during the time of her menses—which is still a "women's issue" in many Orthodox churches.[3]

The works of other authors subsequent to my thesis also have significantly added to and refined points in topics examined herein. I am particularly grateful for research that further explicates Orthodox teaching on sexual differentiation according to the church fathers.[4]

[3]The Letter from Athanasius to Amun, written before AD 354, is a non-conciliar canon, originally written as a private letter but then accepted into the body of canons in Canon II of the Synod in Trullo (Quinisext Council), AD 692. In this long letter are these words: "But when any bodily excretion takes place independently of will, then we experience this, like other things, by a necessity of nature . . . Moreover, one might reasonably say no natural secretion will bring us before Him for punishment . . . What sin, then, is there in God's name, elder most beloved of God, if the Master who made the body willed and made these parts to have such passages?" See Philip Schaff, D.D., L.L.D., and Henry Wace, D.D., eds., *A Select Library of Nicene and Post-Nicene Fathers of the Christian Church,* vol 14, 2nd series (Grand Rapids, MI: Wm. B. Eerdmans Pub. Co., 1892), pp. 602–603. Series hereafter referred to as NPNF. This canonical letter seemingly contradicts another canonical letter, also accepted at the Council of Trullo, that of the Blessed Dionysius, Archbishop of Alexandria, to Basiledes the Bishop. Cf. n. 4 in the Conclusion.

The Letter of St Gregory the Great (AD 540–604) states: ". . . when women after due consideration do not presume to approach the Sacrament of the Body and Blood of the Lord during their courses, they are to be commended. But if they are moved by devout love of this holy mystery to receive it as pious custom suggests, they are not to be discouraged. For while the Old Testament makes outward observances important, the New Testament does not regard these things so highly as the inward disposition, which is the sole true criterion for allotting punishment . . . how can a woman who endures the laws of nature with a pure mind be considered impure?" in *An Ecclesiastical History of the English People,* by the Venerable Bede. Additionally, the First Canon of the Seventh Ecumenical Council states: ". . . the sacred canons are in all things to be observed . . . whether they have been set forth by the Spirit . . . the renowned Apostles . . . the Six Ecumenical Councils . . . by Councils locally assembled for promulgating the decrees of the Ecumenical Councils, or by our holy Fathers. For all these, being illumined by the same Spirit, defined such things as were expedient." In NPNF, vol. 14, second series, p. 555. Cf. n. 5 in the Conclusion.

[4]The Very Rev. Dr John Behr's "A Note on the Ontology of Gender," which carefully explores theological terms relating to sex and gender, and which cautions and instructs researchers in their approach to the writings of church fathers such as St Gregory of Nyssa and St Maximus, in *St Vladimir's Theological Quarterly,* vol. 41, nos. 3 & 4 (1998): pp. 363–372. Also highly instructive is his essay, "The Rational Animal: A Rereading of Gregory of Nyssa's *De Hominis opificio,*" in *Journal of Early Christian Studies* 7:2 (1999): 219–247.

As well, I am thankful for authors who have written about the sacrament of marriage as a Christian vocation.[5]

My wish is that further examination will continue. My lament is that it will continue in a vein—now subtly prevalent—that appropriates the very feminist theology that I rebuffed when I first wrote this little book. My hope is that its re-publication will help readers understand the boundaries of Orthodox teaching, and to realize that boundaries are not necessarily a bad thing: they keep harm out.

A tidal wave of feminist theology has ravaged basic Christian doctrines, leaving them like scattered, twisted driftwood on the seashore. It is time we recall the words of the Lord God in the Book of Job, who says to the raging waves of the sea, "This far you may come, and no farther. And here, your proud waves must stop" (Job 38.10–12).

Our thoughts about God, man, and woman, created and shaped within the set parameters of Orthodox Christian tradition, will be no less true, or no less free, than thoughts that are culturally or philosophically based. For, where the Spirit of the Lord is, *there* is freedom (2 Cor 3.17), and *there* is Truth.

---

[5]The Very Rev. Dr John Breck's insightful examination, "Sexuality, Marriage, and Covenant Responsibility," found in his book *The Sacred Gift of Life: Orthodox Christianity and Bioethics* (Crestwood, NY: St. Vladimir's Seminary Press, 2000), pp. 55–125.

Introduction

The Women's Movement in the United States has had a profound effect on the realm of religion.[1] As the Women's Movement began to be felt in other areas of American life, it soon became apparent that religious structures were not beyond feminist interest.[2] Shortly after the movement began in the early 1960s, feminists decided that sexism had penetrated the Church throughout Christian history, and they judged Christian denominations as having been patently unfair to women. Women began to scrutinize structures of Christian denominations, with their beliefs and theology, and concluded that all of Christendom had been tainted by male chauvinism.

Feminists noted that males usually made up the "power stratum" of the churches; males and only males were usually ordained to be pastor, priest, or bishop. In addition, God was consistently called by "masculine" terms (Father, Son, and Holy Spirit—He), thus making women feel alien to God, while men more easily associated with this "male" God. Women, for the most part, were relegated to less important positions and tasks in churchly gatherings. The churches promoted the idea that the most glorious role a Christian woman could play was that of wife and mother; there was persistent quoting from St Paul's epistles, which urged women to be silent and submissive (e.g., 1 Cor 14.34–36, Eph 5.22).

North American women who had been fighting for liberation, championing women's rights in other aspects of their lives, took their struggles to the doorsteps of their denominations and found that they had entered the most "sexist" area of all! Some left the Chris-

---

[1]Betty Friedan, *It Changed My Life* (New York: Random House, 1963), p. 290.
[2]Mary Daly, *Beyond God the Father: Toward a Philosophy of Women's Liberation* (Boston: Beacon Press, 1973), p. 13.

tian faith, thinking it too archaic and misogynistic. They viewed the church as just another male-dominated institution beyond hope of reform and bent on keeping women weak and reticent.[3] Most feminists, however, stayed within their respective denominations but began to agitate for change. They reviewed church policies, doctrine, Scripture, and liturgical rites and asked for radical transformation in all of these areas.

It must be realized that women who considered themselves both Christian and feminist generally believed that the Christian faith was good, humane, just, and liberating in essence. They reasoned that Jesus Christ had demonstrated an unusually fair policy toward women but that after His death His followers, bound by cultural restrictions in regard to women, had held them back from full participation in the church. They believed that Jesus Christ had intended that Christianity be a faith in which women and men worked in equal partnership but that males in the church had ignored this ideal because they were influenced by the sexist culture around them.[4] Therefore, these feminized-Christians[5] concluded, it was time at last to restore Christianity to the form God had designed for it. Several alterations would be needed to do so.

Feminist theologians propounded that God should be called by feminine as well as masculine names for God. They also began editing the Bible, removing what they felt to be offensive to women by picking up isolated biblical passages and labeling them either as divinely inspired or deformed by cultural influences. The push to

[3]Dr Elizabeth Bettenhausen, professor at Boston University School of Theology, questioned whether "the whole of Christianity has been a religion to reinforce male dominance." See Charles Austin, "Christian Feminists Split on Key Issues in the Church," *New York Times*, March 30, 1981, B-13.

[4]Some feminist theologians feel that cultural influences dampened the spark of freedom intended for all by Jesus Christ and His Spirit, based on such scriptural passages as Gal 5.1 and 3.8. See, for example, Letty Russell, *Human Liberation in a Feminist Perspective—A Theology* (Philadelphia: Westminster Press, 1975), p. 35.

[5]"Feminized-Christians" will be the term used in this paper to designate those believers who have embraced feminist philosophy as the directive of their Christian faith.

advance women to hierarchical rank resulted in the acceptance of the female priesthood by the Episcopal Church in the United States in 1974. In addition, worship services were restructured in order to make them more relevant to women's experiences of life. This is apparent in several feminist writings and books, a typical title being: *Sister Celebrations: Nine Worship Experiences.*[6] Extreme feminists even composed private home rites for worship of the Mother Goddess and the blessing and celebration of womanhood.[7] Further, feminized-Christians studied biblical passages on male-female relationships and concluded that primary and secondary relationships between men and women must be abandoned as "pre-Christian"; they affirmed female-male relational models of equality, outside the influence of stereotypical, culturally-determined roles.

Such propositions are serious because feminized-Christians firmly believe all of these changes accord with the will of God. They signal that the Holy Spirit is hovering over the churches to make them into the new creation promised by Jesus Christ (Rev 21.5).[8] To support their argument, they quote biblical passages like Galatians 3.28: "There is neither Jew nor Greek, there is neither slave nor free, there is neither male nor female; for you are all one in Christ Jesus"; or 2 Corinthians 3.17: "Now the Lord is the Spirit, and where the Spirit of the Lord is, there is freedom." Carter Heywood, one of the women ordained to the Episcopal priesthood in 1974, summed up:

> We put our faith in the power of the Holy Spirit to redeem the structures of the Church so they will more faithfully reflect

[6] Arlene Swidler, ed. (Philadelphia: Fortress Press, 1974).

[7] Zsuzsanna E. Budapest, "Self-Blessing Ritual," in *Womanspirit Rising: A Feminist Reader in Religion*, Carol P. Christ and Judith Plaskow, eds. (New York: Harper & Row, 1979), pp. 269–72.

[8] Feminists who espouse Christianity claim that feminism in fact is an essential element of Christianity. They claim feminism is inherent in the new creation inaugurated by Jesus Christ (2 Cor 5.17). "To be a Christian is to be a feminist," one of my Protestant friends told me.

God's design for the liberation and wholeness of each human being in the world.[9]

Feminized-Christians assert that the church will be washed clean of cultural error, restored to purity, and conformed to divine will only if these challenges by feminist theologians are met.[10]

Such radical claims on such fundamental issues deserve consideration by the Orthodox, especially since the feminist fight for liberty and equality in the Spirit has shaken all of Christendom.[11] One simply has to read news reports about "Equal Rights on the Altar of God"[12] or to note that many denominations are embroiled in revising prayer books and lectionaries to make them less offensive

[9]*A Priest Forever* (New York: Harper & Row, 1976), p. 106.

[10]Feminist theologians often claim that American culture, because of its dualistic, hierarchical power structure, has tended to support and nurture similar sexist attitudes in Christian institutions in the United States, and further, that a sexist Christian theology in the past has in turn been responsible for producing a North American culture which preys on women, the environment, the poor, and the powerless. In other words, American technology and traditional Christian theology are systems that have supported and nurtured each other, but at the same time have led to misogyny, genocide, and the destruction of the natural elements. Therefore, feminist theologians want to purge the churches of these past influences, which have been characterized by racist attitudes, classism, and sexism. See Rosemary Radford Reuther, "Motherearth and Megamachine: A Theology of Liberation in a Feminine, Somatic and Ecological Perspective," in *Womanspirit Rising*. Nevertheless, in this short essay, I submit that feminist theology, likewise, is not a break with the surrounding culture but merely the theology of the liberal end of politics. Theology and culture still are walking hand-in-hand in the feminist movement. Feminized-Christians, it seems, want a new theology but one no less connected to and fed by a modern liberal mindset.

[11]The acceptance of the ordination of women to the priesthood and the widespread publication of feminist theological material give evidence to this fact. Geoffrey W. H. Lampe, D.D., an Anglican professor of divinity at the University of Cambridge, says, "It isn't true, of course, that Rome is solidly against the ordination of women. The declaration of some 1,300 American priests last year (1977) is evidence to the contrary. Many influential Roman theologians support us. Some of the best literature on our side is Roman Catholic." In "A Consideration of Some of the Historical Objections to the Ordination of Women," p. 4: a contributing paper to the debate on this topic held at All Souls, Langham Place, 1978. Professor Lampe and Deaconess McClatchy represented the Anglican group for the Ordination of Women to the Historic Ministry of the Church.

[12]Paul Wilkes, *New York Times Magazine*, November 30, 1980.

to women. (The United Church of Christ has put out guidelines for using inclusive language for God and people, with a list of names other than "Father, Son, and Holy Spirit" one can use for the Deity.)[13] The debate has even invaded popular culture; T-shirts sport the saying, "When God created Adam, She was only fooling."

Therefore, this essay has one purpose: to investigate the religious beliefs of feminized-Christians and to contrast them with Orthodox Christian theology. It is not the desire of the author to depreciate the Women's Movement in other areas of life; in many fields its effects have been beneficial.[14] However, when feminism left social problems and turned to religion, a revolution began, and this revolution has resulted in religious beliefs blatantly disparate with the teachings of the Orthodox Christian Church, with the gospel of Jesus Christ, and with the traditional moving of the Holy Spirit. It is time to analyze the feminized-Christians and their tenets. It is time to decide whether Christianity is undergoing restoration or aberration. To decide, let us consider feminist arguements concerning Scripture, names for God, Jesus Christ, and the General Resurrection.

---

[13]"Inclusive Language Guidelines for Use and Study in the United Church of Christ" (St Louis, MO: Church Leadership Resources, 1980).

[14]Educational and career opportunities now open to women, aid and counseling for battered women and their husbands, and increased bans on pornographic material certainly must be lauded by Christians.

CHAPTER 1

Feminism and the Scriptures

Feminist theologians search the Scriptures for passages they feel have been influenced by patriarchal, male-dominated cultures. Their opposition may be toward the pronouns used in a psalm, a moral teaching, or an illustrative story about a female biblical character. They may take exception, for example, to the line from Psalm 8.4: "What is man that Thou art mindful of him, and the son of man that Thou dost care for him?" Feminized-Christians might want to pray instead, "What is humanity that Thou are mindful of it?" Chapter 5 of Ephesians or chapter 3 of Genesis also might be considered as misogynistic, for the first deals with the submission of a wife to her husband, and the second with the temptation of Eve in the garden. Also abrasive to feminized-Christians are biblical passages about adulteresses and whores (Jn 8 and Rev 17),[1] and passages depicting brutality toward women (Judg 19).

Feminist theologians regard much of Scripture as a reflection of outdated patriarchal societies. Nadine Foley, in her article "Women in Vatican II Documents 1960 to the Present," quotes biblical exegete Raymond Brown as saying:

Since the Bible contains the Word of God in the words of men, these texts reflect the sociology of God's people respec-

---

[1]Feminized-Christians often point out that the Bible gives images of women who are seductive (Gen 3.6, Rev 17) or impossibly pure and virginal—and thus irrelevant to modern women (Lk 1.26–28)—or unclean and impure (Lev 16). However, these images are often simply misinterpretations of the text. See Phyllis Trible, "Eve and Adam: Genesis 2–3 Reread," *Womanspirit Rising*, pp. 74–75.

tively in the first century AD and the eleventh century BC
They cannot be repeated as normative today in a different
sociology without first investigating whether the change of
social condition does not require a different expression of
God's will for His people.

Foley then comments:

This principle certainly applies to the first two chapters of
Genesis so frequently invoked as precedent for a view of
divinely established differences in the nature of men and
women.[2]

Foley's interpretation of Brown's quotation supports, to the
feminist's advantage, the belief that the Bible is a cultural as well as
a divine product. In it are eternal norms and truth; in it also are the
norms and truths of ever-changing human civilization. Following
this premise, feminists argue that since the Bible issued from the
"male mind," it is steeped in male chauvinistic thought patterns.
Therefore, changes in it, whether swapping out a few pronouns or
rewriting an entire passage, are permissible, if not actually essential.
For instance, one feminized-Christian rearranged a well-known
passage from the Book of Job in the following manner:

> I came out of the Mother naked,
> and I will be naked when I return.
> The Mother gave and the Mother takes away,
> I love the Mother.[3]

This is an alteration of the words of the Prophet Job: "Naked I came
from my mother's womb, and naked shall I return; the Lord gave,

[2]James Cordien, ed., *Sexism and Church Law* (New York: Paulist Press, 1977),
p. 102.
[3]Nelle Morton, "The Dilemma of Celebrations," *Womanspirit Rising,* p. 160,
quoting Robert Bly, *Sleepers Joining Hands* (New York: Harper & Row, 1973), p. 31.

and the Lord has taken away; blessed be the name of the Lord" (Job 1.20–22).

Feminists neither agree which scriptural passages should be revised nor how they should be revised, but they are in general agreement on one point: Scripture is written in human words—more specifically, in male words—and is therefore subject to error and open to correction.

The traditional Orthodox Christian view of Scripture challenges this premise. True, Scripture is written in human words (for how else would humans understand God?), but in words divinely revealed. These human words, out of all human words in the world, not only are inspired by God but also connect us to God as we meditate upon them.

Twentieth-century Orthodox theologian Georges Florovsky wrote:

> . . . when divine truths are expressed in human language, the words themselves are transformed . . . . *The Word of God is not diminished when it resounds in human language. On the contrary the human word is transformed, and as it were, transfigured* because of the fact that it pleased God to speak in a human language.[4]

Words in the Bible are not sprung from the human imagination or from human wisdom (or from human depravity); rather, they are put into the hearts and minds of humans by the Spirit of God. In Orthodox Christian tradition, the words of the Bible are not subject willy-nilly to change, because they are words inspired by the Holy Spirit.[5] And ultimately, all words of Scripture point to the Word Himself, Jesus Christ (Jn 5.39–41).

[4]Georges Florovsky, *Creation and Redemption: Volume Three in the Collected Works of Georges Florovsky* (Belmont, MA: Nordland Pub. Co., 1976), pp. 24–25.

[5]Thomas Hopko, *Bible and Church History: An Elementary Handbook on the Orthodox Church,* vol. 3, 2nd ed. (Syosset, NY: Department of Religious Education, Orthodox Church in America, 1979), p. 6.

If, however, one accepts the feminist premise and opens Scripture to subjective and evolving revision, one in effect admits that anyone with a "cause" would be able to rewrite Scripture at whim: from age to age Christians could compose Scripture according to the cultural mores or philosophy in vogue. One also in effect admits that only certain Scriptures have been inspired by the Spirit of God; others have not.

Further, acceptance of this feminist premise is tantamount to saying that when the Church sorted ancient spiritual writings and placed some of them into the biblical canon, the Holy Spirit was ineffectual: a male-dominated hierarchy made mistakes in choosing which writings were divinely inspired, and the Spirit of God was unable at that time to overcome their cultural convictions. Ultimately, acceptance of the feminist premise amounts to an admission that the Bible is the invention of the male mind and not a divinely inspired group of writings—and, more seriously—that the Bible's ancient words, written in an ancient culture, remain relevant only if revised in accordance with the cultural milieu of each age.

This radical admission is welcomed by many feminized-Christians. The consequences of such an admission, however, would result in drastic changes to the shape of Scripture. The New Testament would be greatly altered because of the numerous references to the "Father" and "Son," not only in the Gospels but in most of St Paul's Epistles as well.

Also, it seems unlikely that the vast range of feminist thought would allow for uniformity of Scripture. Some feminists would prefer changes in certain passages, while others would not. In the end, the Bible would cease to be a consistent reference among Christian denominations: not only would it be interpreted differently (a problem present before the Women's Movement began) but there also would be different words to interpret!

This clamor is unnecessary. One has only to peruse the Bible itself to conclude it is not an invention of the male mind designed to subdue or insult women: in it are passages that exult both women and men and in it are passages that deride women and men. For example, praise for Judith, a brave Jewess, is glorious following her victory over the captain of the Assyrian army:

> Then Joakim the high priest, and the senate of the people of Israel who lived at Jerusalem, came to witness the good things which the Lord had done for Israel, and to see Judith and to greet her. And when they met her they all blessed her with one accord and said to her, "You are the exaltation of Jerusalem, you are the great glory of Israel, you are the great pride of our nation! You have done all this singlehanded; you have done great good to Israel, and God is well pleased with it. May the Almighty Lord bless you for ever!" And all the people said, "So be it!"
>
> Then all the women of Israel gathered to see her, and blessed her, and some of them performed a dance for her; and she took branches in her hands and gave them to the women who were with her; and they crowned themselves with olive wreaths . . . and she went before all the people in the dance, leading all the women, while all the men of Israel followed, bearing their arms and wearing garlands and with songs on their lips (Jdt 15.8–10, 12–13).

Clearly, Scripture honors women for bravery and wisdom (Judg 4 and 5; 2 Kg 22.14–20), as well as for being righteous wives and mothers (1 Pet 3.1–6; Prov 31). Some females in the Bible are depicted as wanton, but others are shown to be helpers and persons of inspiration (Rom 16; Acts 18.26).

Further, many biblical passages negatively portray men. Feminists often complain that women in Scripture are at times described as "unclean" because of their monthly menstrual cycle. However, they fail to mention that emissions of semen from male bodies also were labeled "unclean" in Jewish tradition:

> And if a man has an emission of semen, he shall bathe his
> whole body in water, and be unclean until the evening. And
> every garment and every skin on which the semen comes
> shall be washed with water, and be unclean until the evening.
> If a man lies with a woman and has an emission of semen,
> both of them shall bathe themselves in water, and be unclean
> until the evening (Lev 15.16–18).

Thus, men with natural bodily discharges were ritually unclean, just as were women with natural bodily discharges.[6]

In addition, males were often the subjects of brutality in the Bible, as were women. Feminists point to the degraded position of women in Judges 19, in which a Levite, to save himself from homosexual rape, throws his concubine to the base men of Gibeah who gang-rape her to death. Then her owner-husband cuts her into pieces and sends her severed body to the twelve tribes as an example of this abomination. In chapter 20 the Gibeonites are put to the sword and their town burned. The brutality toward the woman is extreme, but times were not, in general, gentle. The book of Judges closes with the explanation that "in those days there was no king in Israel; every man did what was right in his own eyes" (21.25).

The kings themselves, when they came, were equally brutal to both sexes. Saul massacred the priests of the Lord with their entire town, "both men and women, children and sucklings, oxen, asses and sheep," because Ahimelech the priest had helped David (as he had often done before), not knowing that he was fleeing from Saul (1 Sam 22.9–19). David had his loyal servant Uriah the Hittite slain, because Uriah possessed a beautiful wife, whom David had seduced and impregnated (2 Sam 11). Jehu had the seventy young

---

[6]The term "uncleaness" as used in the Old Testament does not refer primarily to personal hygiene, nor to personal sinfulness. Rather, it is used in a cultic sense. There was a certain aura about a man emitting semen or woman issuing blood, as well as a "loss of vitality, a diminution of the life principle . . . ," and this resulted in exclusion from cultic worship. See *The Jerome Biblical Commentary,* Raymond E. Brown, S.S., et al., eds. (Englewood Cliffs, NJ: Prentice Hall, 1968), p. 76, commentary on *Leviticus.*

sons of Ahab—no mention of his daughters—murdered, their heads brought to him in basketsful and exhibited in two heaps by the city gates (2 Kg 10).

Nor was it only men who shed blood without compunction. Athaliah, mother of king Ahaziah of Judah, "was her son's counselor in doing wickedly" (2 Chr 22.3). When Jehu killed Ahaziah and Athaliah "saw that her son was dead, she arose and destroyed all the royal family of the house of Judah." The only one of her grandsons that survived was the infant Joash, because his aunt, Athaliah's daughter Jehoshabeath, "stole him away from among the king's sons"—again, not his daughters—"who were about to be slain" (2 Chr 22.10–12).

Furthermore, as far as sexual sins against women are concerned, Deuteronomy 22.23–24 is unambiguous: when a man rapes a virgin, the crime is his alone and he must die—a welcome change from the contemporary attitude that "she got what was coming to her; she led him on." God Himself punished David for his sin with Bathsheba (2 Sam 12). There is no double standard in Scripture: adultery is a sin for men and women alike (Lev 20; Mk 10.11–12; 1 Cor 6.9–10).

Scripture records good men and evil men, good women and evil women; it shows base depravity as it occurred and gives glorious honor where it is deserved, regardless of sex. The feminist argument that the Bible was designed by males to warp women's minds or to portray them as basically despicable is not plausible. Scripture is the record of continuing salvation history, which is consummated when the Son of God is born of a woman (Gal 4.4).

In Orthodox Christian tradition the Bible has been revered by female as well as male saints, as food from the Holy Spirit that has nourished their souls. St Macrina, a famous Orthodox saint of the fourth century wrote:

> . . . we make the Holy Scripture the rule and measure of every tenet; we necessarily fix our eyes upon that, and approve that

alone which may be made to harmonize with the intention of those writings.[7]

Ironically, St Macrina wrote this to her brother, St Gregory of Nyssa, concerning the doctrine of the resurrection from the dead. Macrina was using Scripture as her rule and guide in the debate; her brother was using arguments from Greek philosophy. Macrina reproved him for relying on Hellenistic thought and admonished him to depend instead on Scripture for instruction in the matter at hand.

Clearly, St Macrina considered Scripture as divinely inspired, as opposed to the culturally and humanly inspired words of Greek wisdom. Regrettably, Christian women today are failing to have the courage and insight of St Macrina, for they do not rely on the Holy Bible in the face of a new philosophy, feminism.

[7]NPNF, second series, vol 5, p. 439.

CHAPTER 2

Feminism and the Holy Trinity

Just as feminists in the United States are trying to rid the English language of "sexist" terms and slogans—e.g., changing "Men Working" to "Crews Working"—so feminist theologians are advocating changes in terminology for God. They reject "Father, Son, and Holy Spirit," which connote masculine images, and prefer terms such as "Parent," "Mother," "Fire," "Light," and so forth.[1]

Yet for centuries, Christians have called upon God as "Father." Why? Feminist theologians have attributed this traditional term to several factors, such as:

1) God naturally was named by a "masculine" term because only males were allowed to develop doctrinal teachings. It would be advantageous to males to construct a theology of a "masculine" God to strengthen their own dominant position in society; women would fall third in the line of succession of power: God, man, and woman. Males, being more apparently "in the image" of the God worshipped, would be able to claim superiority and lordship over women, who would be more alienated, by their sex and gender, from the divine power.[2]

In short, male terms for God were used as a device to keep women separated from the realm of religion and to keep them silent and submissive, while insisting a "masculine" God had ordered them to be so.

2) God has been named only in male terms because women have been prevented from presenting their perceptions of God. The male

---

[1]"Inclusive Language Guidelines for the United Church of Christ," p. 14.
[2]Daly, *Beyond God the Father*, p. 13.

terms are not an ingenious powerplay but merely an oversight. Since only males expressed their ideas about the Deity, only the masculine point of view was presented, making for a "lopsided" God. If only males were making theological statements, naturally the Deity was viewed as the prototype of men only.[3]

When females begin to theologize, they will perceive God as the prototype of themselves, that is, feminine. When the views of humanity in total are considered, God will become holistic, the archetype of both male and female. God will be known as both "Father" and "Mother."

3) Calling God "Father" was only a biological misunderstanding! In ancient times people were unaware of the biological processes involved in the creation of human life. They thought that the father was the source of a child's life, and that the mother was merely a passive vessel in which to carry the fetus. All of life sprang from the male, and the seed he planted in the female grew to perfection in her without any significant biological contribution from her. Therefore, the ultimate Source of all life was called "Father" and not mother.[4]

Nowadays people know that a sperm from the male and an egg from the female create life, therefore allowing reference to the Source of all life as both "Father" and "Mother."

4) In pre-biblical times God was worshipped not as one but as two strong deities, one masculine and one feminine—the Father Sky-God and the Mother Goddess—who cooperatively ruled the earth. These two deities were adored at a time when men and women equally cooperated in the performance of daily, vital tasks. However, when cultural conditions changed (especially among the Hebrews)

[3]"Women doing theology are increasingly determined to rely on their own experience as reliable data, often against a doctrinal ecclesiology which is determined to set the perimeters of valid discovery." In Dody H. Donnelly, "Why Ordain Anybody—for awhile?" *Cross Currents* 27 (Summer 1978), p. 140.

[4]As expressed at a World Council of Churches consultation: "The Ordination of Women in Ecumenical Perspective," held at Chateau Klingenthal, France, 1979. Referred to in the booklet emerging from that consultation: *Ordination of Women in Ecumenical Perspective*, ed. Constance Parvey, Faith and Order Paper 105 (Geneva: World Council of Churches, 1980), p. 57.

and males became socially dominant, the image of the Mother Goddess was repressed and the image of the Father Sky-God was elevated.[5]

Now, both Judaism and Christianity, having suppressed the Goddess, must "repent," and revitalize her as a deity concerned with the motherly tasks of helping the poor, relieving the oppressed, and preserving the resources of the earth.

5) The names of God given by Jesus Christ (Jn 14) were not divinely revealed. Jesus was a first-century male influenced by the surrounding culture. He had His own spirituality that need not influence other individuals. He wanted to refer to God as "Father," but this name need not be normative for others. He held His own special view of God, and others should be free to express their views of God as well.[6]

6) Certain biblical passages portray God using a motherly image (Is 46.3–4; Ps 131.1–2; Lk 13.34), and church fathers and mystics (both women and men) have written about God as "Mother." A male-oriented hierarchy has overlooked these images because of prejudice, and now mother imagery should be restored, having always been present in the Christian tradition.[7]

7) Since God is spirit (Jn 4.24), neither masculine nor feminine terms should be used. Impersonal, neuter terms such as "Creator,

---

[5]A description of these cosmic deities is found in Mircea Eliade, *The Sacred and The Profane* (New York: Harcourt, Brace & World, 1959), pp. 116ff. Rosemary Ruether makes reference to this phenomenon in "Motherearth and Megamachine," *Womanspirit Rising*, pp. 47ff.

[6]Such an opinion was expressed by Ada Maria Isasi-Dias in a keynote address, "On Gathering Our Sustenance, Strategizing for Action, and Maintaining Our Hope," at a Women's Interseminary Conference, February 20–22, 1981, held at Union Theological Seminary, New York City.

[7]There are many patristic, as well as mystic writings in which God is viewed as a mother, both in Eastern Orthodox and Western Christianity. For example, St Therese of Lisieux, a Roman Catholic nun of the Carmelite order, wrote in the nineteenth century: "I know that God loves us more tenderly than any mother, and is a mother not always ready to forgive the involuntary little failings of her child?" Christopher O'Mahoney, O.C.D., ed., *St Therese of Lisieux by Those Who Knew Her* (Noll Plaza, Huntington, IN: *Our Sunday Visitor*, 1975), p. 43.

Savior, and Sanctifier" would be better than the trinitarian names, "Father, Son, and Holy Spirit."

We need not view God as three persons but as active forces, using names such as "God-the Verb" to denote motion, power, and fluidity.[8]

An Orthodox Response

How might an Orthodox Christian respond to these feminist arguments? Let's take them one by one.

The first argument assumes that a patriarchal culture produced a male/masculine image of God in order to support a religious system that kept women in second place.

Upon consideration this seems highly doubtful. Patriarchal cultures that surrounded the Hebrews nevertheless adored both female and male deities. Likewise, early Christians in male-dominated cultures were surrounded by pagans that worshipped female deities (Acts 19). It seems Jews and Christians were under no cultural obligation to refer to God in masculine terms.

Additionally, neither Jews nor Christians ever thought of God as comparable to male human beings. The Bible had warned the Hebrews to think of God as neither male nor female:

> Since you saw no form on the day that the Lord spoke to you at Horeb out of the midst of the fire, beware lest you act corruptly by making a graven image for yourselves, in the form of any figure, the likeness of male or female . . . (Deut 4.15–16).

Rarely in the Old Testament is God referred to as "Father." Rather, He was Yahweh, the indescribable "I Am Who I Am" (Ex 3.14). Jesus

---

[8]Alla Bozarth-Campbell, *Womanpriest: A Personal Odyssey* (New York: Paulist Press, 1978), pp. 198ff.

Himself told His followers that God is spirit, not a sexed creature (Jn 4.24).

Moreover, both Jews and Christians, unlike the surrounding society, treated women more fairly than cultural custom and law would allow. St Gregory Nazianzen, for example, discussed the double standard of the civil law and admonished Christians regarding it:

> [Let me discuss] chastity, in respect of which I see that the majority of men are ill-disposed, and that their laws are unequal and irregular. For what was the reason why they restrained the woman, but indulged the man, and that a woman who practices evil against her husband's bed is an adulteress, and the penalties of the law for this are very severe; but if the husband commits fornication against his wife, he has no account to give? I do not accept this legislation; I do not approve this custom. Those who made the law were men, and therefore the legislation is hard on women.[9]

St Gregory did not agree with the male chauvinistic attitudes of society, yet he worshipped God as Father, Son, and Holy Spirit, and even wrote some of his best orations on the Holy Trinity.[10] His argumentation hints that a patriarchal culture was not responsible for "male" terminology for God; the Trinitarian names have deeper meaning (which we will discuss shortly). The feminist link between patriarchal culture and male imagery or masculine names for the Deity seems weak.

The second argument states that women have not had an opportunity to name God. Two outstanding examples of Orthodox women saints could refute their claim.

The aforementioned St Macrina, sister to two great Orthodox theologians, St Basil the Great and St Gregory of Nyssa, was referred

---

[9]"On Words of the Gospel," NPNF, vol. 7, p. 339.
[10]Ibid., see summary of Gregory's theological orations, NPNF, vol. 7, p.200.

to by her brothers as the "Teacher."[11] She had raised them in the faith and instructed them in the theology of the Father, Son, and Holy Spirit. No one had forced her to do so.

Likewise, St Nina, Evangelizer of the Georgians, converted that entire nation to Christianity, to belief in Jesus Christ and the Holy Trinity: Father, Son, and Holy Spirit.[12] She did so of her own volition; she had not been commissioned by the male hierarchy. Even as a slave in a foreign country she proclaimed what she believed.

These female saints had exactly the same vision of God as male Christians. Neither one had been brainwashed or compelled to believe in God as Father, Son, and Holy Spirit. Their theology was compatible with the rest of the Church. Given their legacy, it would be inaccurate to claim that women have never had the opportunity to teach or to contribute to theological thought or to proclaim the Good News of God.[13]

The feminist assumption that women as women, when moved by the Holy Spirit will perceive God in a different, "feminine" manner is not necessarily true. Women in other fields may have made great contributions by offering the "woman's point of view" (e.g., in journalism, law enforcement, medicine, politics), but the same cannot be said of the field of theology, because God is not determined by human thought and reasoning. According to Orthodox Christian tradition and the Bible (Ex 3; 1 Kg 19.11–13; Is 6.1–3), God reveals Himself objectively. The Holy Spirit reveals God (1 Cor 2.10–13), and the Holy Spirit does not reveal one type of God to males and another type to females. St Paul says, "There is one body and one Spirit . . .

---

[11]"On the Soul and the Resurrection," NPNF, vol. 5, pp. 430ff.

[12]*The Life of St Nina Equal to the Apostles and Enlightener of Georgia* [with the service to her life included] (Jordanville, NY: Holy Trinity Russian Orthodox Monastery, 1977).

[13]Some feminized-Christians agree that women have had opportunities to contemplate God and to record their own writings, but they still regret that such saints never were part of the official magisterium of the Church. See Rosemary Ruether, "Mothers of the Church: Ascetic Women in the Late Patristic Age," in *Women of Spirit*, ed. Rosemary Ruether and Eleanor McLaughlin (New York: Simon & Schuster, 1979), p. 94.

one Lord, one faith, one baptism, one God and Father of us all, who is above all and through all and in all" (Eph 4.4–6). Women and men in the Church who have acquired sainthood and who knew the one, true God as perfectly as humanly possible did not receive conflicting or partial images depending upon their sex.[14] They all accepted the traditional names for God: Father, Son, and Holy Spirit.

Argument number three—the "biological argument"—can also be put to rest in quick order. Historical evidence shows that early Christians could indeed have known some intricacies of human procreation, but they nevertheless referred to God as "Father." For example, St John Chrysostom, in the fourth century, wrote in his Homily XX on Ephesians 5.31:

> . . . a man leaving them that begat him, and from whom he was born, is knit to his wife; and that then the one flesh is, father, and mother, and the child, from the substance of the two commingled. For indeed, by the commingling of their seeds is the child produced, so that the three are one flesh . . . Because so it has been from the beginning.[15]

[14]This is not to say that God is completely "knowable" or "known," for the Orthodox Christian Divine Liturgy (eucharistic service) always proclaims God as "ineffable, inconceivable, invisible, incomprehensible, ever-existing and eternally the same . . ." Nevertheless, Orthodox Christians would say that the revelation of God as Father, Son, and Holy Spirit in the New Testament (Mt 3.16–17) is normative for Christians today—male or female.

Twentieth-century Orthodox Christian theologian Vladimir Lossky explained the different methods of "knowing God" in *The Mystical Theology of the Eastern Church* (Crestwood, NY: St Vladimir's Seminary Press, 1980), pp. 114–15: "St Augustine takes as his starting point the image of God in man, and attempts to work out an idea of God, by trying to discover in Him that which we find in the soul created in His image. The method he employs is one of psychological analogies applied to the knowledge of God, to theology. On the other hand, St Gregory of Nyssa [Eastern tradition], for instance, starts with what the revelation tells us of God in order to discover what it is in man which corresponds to the divine image. This is a theological method applied to the knowledge of God to man, to anthropology. The first way seeks to know God by starting from man created in his image; the second wishes to define the true nature of man by starting from the idea of God in whose image man has been created." In his work, Lossky stressed the importance of "starting from the idea of God."

[15]NPNF, vol. 13, first series, p. 146.

According to St John, the seed of the mother played an equal part in reproduction, yet the Source of all life was called by him "Father" and not "Mother."

The fourth argument presumes that "Father God" imagery supports a male-dominated society that cares little for the "feminine" virtues of love, mercy, and tenderness and that does not identify with the oppressed or have concern for all forms of life. The God of the Bible, however, shows loving-kindness and care for the earth:

> Can a woman forget her sucking child, that she should have no compassion on the son of her womb? Even these may forget, yet I will not forget you (Is 49.15).

> Thou makest springs gush forth in the valleys; they flow between the hills, they give drink to every beast of the field; the wild asses quench their thirst. By them the birds of the air have their habitation; they sing among the branches. From Thy lofty abode Thou waterest the mountains; the earth is satisfied with the fruit of Thy work (Ps 104.10–13, and entire Psalm).

This God, spouse of the Hebrew bride, has more tenderness than a new mother, and more concern for creation than any human being.

Likewise, in the New Testament, Jesus reveals His Father's love:

"As the Father has loved Me, so have I loved you; abide in My love" (Jn 15.9).

The love of Jesus and His Father was a sacrificial love beyond human understanding. Even though called by a masculine name, "Abba," Jesus' God did not fail in love and compassion for all creatures.

The fifth argument insinuates that Jesus Christ is a human being and not of God. Some feminist theologians do perceive Jesus as little more than a good human being—inspired perhaps, but just

as inspired as others. Many feminist theologians are further willing
to equate the male Christ of Christianity with one of the ancient
goddesses:

> . . . there is a self-conscious exploration into ancient myth,
> symbol, and archetype going on among feminist artists,
> writers, psychologists and theologians. In their experience
> the ancient mother Goddesses are being resurrected and are
> demonstrating that their formative and integrative powers
> are equal to that of the Christ.[16]

This fifth argument, in denying that Jesus is the one incarnate Word
of God, completely opposes Orthodox Christian doctrine and the
Nicene Creed.

Interestingly, argument six—the use of motherly imagery for
God—includes some points of agreement between feminist theologians and Orthodox Christianity, particularly when speaking about
the Holy Spirit, the third person of the Holy Trinity. A few twentieth-century theologians have perceived the Holy Spirit as possessing and
demonstrating "feminine" qualities, and have even gone so far as to
say that the Holy Spirit is an archetypal pattern for women. Why?

The Holy Spirit brings to fruition the will of God (Lk 1.35) and
is closely associated with motherhood, comfort and counsel (Jn
16.1–15). Therefore, the Holy Spirit is sometimes viewed as expressing a "feminine" mode of life. This is not to say that the Holy Spirit is
"female." The twentieth-century Orthodox scholar Vladimir Lossky
states:

> The Fathers relate the procession of the Holy Spirit with what
> they call the "procession" of Eve, different from Adam yet of
> the same nature as him: unity of nature and plurality of persons evoke for us the mysteries of the New Testament. Just as

---

[16]Sheila Collins, "Reflections on the Meaning of Herstory," in *Womanspirit Rising*, p. 71.

the Spirit is not inferior to Him from whom it proceeds, just
so woman is not inferior to man: for love demands equality
and love alone wished this primordial polarization, source of
all diversity of the human species.[17]

Likewise, Fr Thomas Hopko presses the point:

I believe that God created human beings according to his
own image and likeness because of the trinitarian character
of the Divine Nature, and that *the proper interrelationship
between the sexes within the order of creation is patterned
after the interrelationship between God's Son and his Spirit.*
The divine interrelationship is the "prototype" of the union
between a man and a woman in the community of marriage.
I would only offer on this point, admittedly undeveloped in
Christian theology, the fact that the holy fathers, particularly
St Gregory the Theologian, insist that the Godhead is not
merely a "unity" but a "union." Within this "union" there is
a definite "order" of relationships, which is perfectly divine,
yet which includes a distinction of personal "modes of existence" in which the Son and the Spirit have a definite form
of relationship . . . [emphasis mine].[18]

Curiously, Scripture states:

. . . she is a breath of the power of God, and a pure emanation
of the glory of the Almighty . . . (Wis 7.25).

Thus, in Scripture and in theological writings, a feminine principle in God has been perceived. However—and here the feminist
and Orthodox theologians part company—this feminine prin-

---

[17]*Orthodox Theology: An Introduction* (Crestwood, NY: St Vladimir's Seminary
Press, 1978), pp. 69–70.
    [18]*The Spirit of God* (Wilton, CT: Morehouse-Barlow Co., 1976), pp. 49–50.

ciple is linked with the third person of the Trinity, the Holy Spirit; there would be no justification to call God the Father, "God the Mother."[19]

The seventh and final feminist argument presupposes that fleshly, human terms such as "Father" and "Son" should not be applied to God who is spirit. Therefore, words like "Creator, Savior, and Sanctifier" are preferred to "Father, Son, and Holy Spirit."

Ironically, this is an old argument, originally put forward by men! In the fourth century during the Arian controversy St Athanasius faced this same argument. Here's how the debate ensued.

A group within the Church, the Arians, refused to call God "Father" because they felt the term to be fleshly and foolish.[20] If God were a father, they reasoned, could he someday be a grandfather? And where was the mother within this Triune God? Arians felt it unwise to use such a term and preferred calling God "Creator" instead. (It is tempting to mention that these Arians were all male theologians, so apparently the insistence of the Church on the term "Father" was not a patriarchal ploy or a mark of male solidarity.)

St Athanasius set out to argue logically with the Arians. Using a term such as "Creator," he said, makes God dependent on creatures for His existence. If there were no creatures, would the Creator cease to be? (Likewise, if there were no sinners, would the Savior cease to be? Or if there were no saints, whom would the Sanctifier purify?) Athanasius explained that these neutral terms do well to describe the actions of God, but they are useless in describing the Trinity and the loving relationship among the three persons that existed before the creation of humanity.

Additionally, Athanasius argued, the words "Creator, Savior, and Sanctifier" could be used to describe any one of the three members

---

[19]Joan Schaupp, *Woman: Image of the Holy Spirit* (Denville, NJ: Dimension Books, 1975). Naming the first person of the Trinity "Mother" does occur in poetical, mystical Christian writings, as differentiated from the doctrinal terms of "Father, Son and Holy Spirit." Cf. n. 28.

[20]For a historical explanation of this heresy see Philip Schaff, *History of the Christian Church*, Vol. 3 (Grand Rapids, MI: Eerdmans Pub. Co., 1910), pp. 618–49.

of the Trinity: how then could anyone know to which person one was referring?[21] It would be wrong to refer to the Father alone as "Creator," because the Bible states (concerning the Spirit and Son respectively):

In the beginning God created the heavens and earth. The earth was without form and void, and darkness was upon the face of the deep; and the Spirit of God was moving over the face of the waters (Gen 1.1–2).

In the beginning was the Word, and the Word was with God, and the Word was God. He was in the beginning with God; all things were made through Him, and without Him was not anything made that was made (Jn 1.1–3).

In Orthodox Christian thought and according to the Bible, the Trinity acts in concert. They all create. They all save (Jn 5.21; Acts 2.24; Rom 1.4). They all sanctify (Eph 5.26; 1 Thess 5.23). They are all holy, good, and divine. These neutral terms describe merely how God acts toward creatures; they do not adequately describe how the Trinity exists as three persons in a relationship. They describe actions of God but do not differentiate among the persons. Therefore, the Orthodox Church regards them as imperfect compared to the personal names of "Father, Son, and Holy Spirit."

Traditionally God is not regarded as a force or action or a "verb" rather than three persons. Again, Vladimir Lossky states:

[God] is a personal Absolute who enters into relationships with human persons. For Judaism before Christ, as for the believing Jew today, this is so. To quote the witness of Martin Buber: "The great achievement of Israel is not to have taught

---

[21]For Athanasius' arguments see *Contra Arianos,* 1.33, as explained by Florovsky in *Aspects of Church History: Volume Four in the Collected Works of Georges Florovsky* (Belmont, MA: Nordland Pub. Co., 1975), pp. 52ff.

the one true God, who is the only God, the source and end of all that is; it is to have shown that it was possible in reality to speak to Him, to say 'Thou' to Him, to stand upright before His face."[22]

God is three persons *who relate to each other* as Father, Son, and Spirit, and God speaks and interacts with human beings.[23] Thus, two types of terminology for God are needed: personal names and descriptive nouns. However, these two types are not equal or interchangeable: one set of terms helps us understand the internal relationships among the members of the Holy Trinity and their personal characteristics; the other set of terms tells us how God acts towards us creatures.

God, our Father

This section would not be complete without some explanation as to why the Church consistently has used the term "Father" for the first person of the Trinity. St Gregory of Nyssa, already mentioned, elucidates this point.

First, says St Gregory, this term was given to us by Jesus Christ—whom he calls "the best theologian."[24] By studying this name we learn about the character of God and Trinitarian life. We receive intimations as to the personal qualities of the First Person of the Trinity, and how He relates to the Son and Spirit. Although "Father, Son, and Holy Spirit" are only human terms, they are the most adequate human terms available to describe God.[25]

---

[22]*In the Image and Likeness of God* (Crestwood, NY: St Vladimir's Seminary Press, 1974), p. 129.

[23]The depersonalization of names for God has led to a depersonalization of God. Ruth Tiffany Barnhouse, in *Women and Orders*, Robert J. Heyer, ed. (New York: Paulist Press, 1974), p. 21, expresses this: " . . . in order to establish a living relationship with God, we behave *as though* God were a person" (emphasis mine).

[24]"Against Eunomius," book I, in NPNF, vol. 5, p. 53.

[25]Ibid., book II, 2, p. 102.

The word "Father" denotes two things: 1) there is a child involved and this child existed with a timeless parent from all eternity; and 2) this person, like a human father, is the initiator of a generation, the inaugurator, and one who begets life rather than bringing it to fruition in birth.[26] Nowhere does St Gregory suggest that the Father is male from the human standpoint. He notes: "It is clear that this metaphor contains a deeper meaning than the obvious one . . ."[27]

This "deeper meaning" may be found in a passage of St Paul to the Ephesians:

> For this reason I bow my knees before the Father, from whom every family [lit., fatherhood: πατριά] in heaven and on earth is named . . . (Eph. 3.14–15).[28]

St Gregory implies that God is the one, true, divine Father, whom human fathers imitate in a creaturely, imperfect way.[29] Orthodox Christians do not call God "Father" to justify a patriarchal culture. Rather, males in a human household are called "fathers" because they imitate the fatherhood of our heavenly Father.[30] Males have not constructed a "male God" and foisted Him on women. Rather, our

[26]Feminists argue that woman, as well as man, is the source of all life, therefore, this first person of the Trinity may be called "Mother" as well as "Father." The early Church was well aware that both male and female cells contributed to the creation of life (cf. n. 15), however, the Church also maintained a distinction between begetting and bearing, between the male and female contributions and the mode of action in creating life. It is the male sperm that is the generator, the inaugurator and impregnator of the female egg. There is a biological distinction, even at this basic level, between being father or mother.

[27]"Against Eunomius," book I, 23 in NPNF, vol. 5, p. 63.

[28]St Gregory comments on this eternal Fatherhood: "Just, then, as we cannot say that God was never good, nor powerful, nor imperishable, nor immortal, in the same way it is blasphemy not to attribute to Him Fatherhood always, and to say that that came later. He Who is truly Father is always Father. . . ." Ibid., book I, 38 in NPNF, vol. 5, p. 90.

[29]Louis Bouyer, *Woman in the Church* (San Francisco: Ignatius Press, 1979), p. 35.

[30]Thomas Hopko, ed., *Women and Men in the Church* (Syosset, NY: Department of Religious Education, Orthodox Church in America, 1980), pp. 12–13.

heavenly Father exists as an objective reality, and fathers on earth, insofar as they possess His generative function and exercise fatherhood, mirror His way of life.

God is beyond sex, and God's eternal, divine fatherhood is as distant from creaturely fatherhood as God is from the creature. St Gregory explains:

> . . . each one of these names [Father, Son, and Holy Spirit] has a human sound, but not a human meaning, so also that of Father, while applying equally to life divine and human, hides a distinction between the uttered meanings exactly proportionate to the difference existing between the subjects of this title. We think of man's generation one way; we surmise the divine generation in another.[31]

Jesus Christ Himself suggested the vast divide between earthly and divine fatherhood:

> And call no man your father on earth, for you have one Father, who is in heaven (Mt 23.9).

Yet, Jesus Christ consistently called God "Father" and not "Mother." The Lord recognized the fatherhood of God in its divine, perfect form: before time, within the mystery of the Holy Trinity, His Father generated a Son. The best human term possible to describe this eternal, divine, generative action was employed by Jesus Christ: "Father."[32]

---

[31]"Against Eunomius," book I, 39 in NPNF, vol. 5, p. 93.

[32]Gail R. Schmidt, "Lutheran Liturgical Prayer and God as Mother," *Worship* 52:6 (November 1978), pp. 517–542, adds another sound theological reason why Jesus consistently refers to God as "Father." She states that Jesus claimed to be the Chosen one of God, since the word "Father" in reference to God could be used only by a covenanted people. This intimate address by Jesus Himself had a concept of God as progenitor; this seminal image of God as "Father" is first written about in the Gospel of John (Jn 1.8; 1.14; 16.28).

This divine Father is as different from earthly fathers as the divine is from the human, nevertheless fatherhood, not motherhood, describes His mode of life, His relation to the second person of the Trinity, and to the children of God through Jesus Christ (1 Jn 1.3).

Moreover, the first person of the Trinity does not just "act" like a father (though He sometimes acts like a mother!); His very being expresses perfect fatherhood. Fatherhood may amount to a creative function of males on earth, or men may take on a fatherly, protective role within the family. However, for the first person of the Trinity, fatherhood is the principle of His being. The Father is fatherhood personified.[33] God is not male, but God is Father. Although it is permissible according to Orthodox tradition to use the term "Mother" poetically or to use motherly imagery for God (e.g., Is 46.3–4), "Father" is the only proper divine name for the first person of the Trinity.

Theological contemplation is difficult, but such difficulty only highlights the serious problem with using names and terms for God indiscriminately. There is a modern opinion, widespread in the United States, that it really does not matter how one views God, since God is unknowable and incomprehensible. This opinion, however, has no place within the true Christian faith. Women and men in the early Church received a revelation of God (Acts 2.17–21); females and males experienced and viewed God as Father, Son, and Holy Spirit and taught others so (Rom 16). In the twentieth century as well Christians must accept this revelation of the one, true God, and of the names that most perfectly describe the Deity. Says St Gregory emphatically: "Any other terms would lead to a deflection of sound doctrine."[34]

---

[33]Louis Boyer, *Woman in the Church*, p. 32: "In case of the heavenly father, Fatherhood is much more than a function: it is a subsistent relationship by virtue of which everything subsists which shall subsist."

[34]St Gregory of Nyssa, "Against Eunomius," book II, 9 in NPNF, vol. 5, p. 116.

CHAPTER 3

Feminism and Jesus Christ

Not only are feminized-Christians concerned with the image of the first person of the Trinity, they are disturbed by the image of Jesus Christ as well. Because He is male and the central figure of the Christian faith, Jesus is an embarrassment to feminist theologians who try to justify their beliefs to feminist colleagues. Radical feminists have even left their churches because the Christian religion has at its foundation a male human being.

However, feminists unwilling to take such a drastic step have studied the "problem of the male Jesus" and have come up with a solution to settle any suspicion that Christianity is a religion for males only: de-emphasize the maleness of Jesus Christ and emphasize His common humanity. Feminist theologians are spreading the message of a de-sexed, ungendered Jesus.

Asexual Heavenly Bliss

Proponents of the Women's Movement actively try to break down stereotypical images of women and men to minimize differences between the sexes. Radical feminists claim there are no psychological differences between men and women, that there is no innately masculine or feminine character, and that the differences between women and men are purely anatomical.[1] Men and women have been culturally conditioned to behave certain ways, they say, but these

---

[1]Walter L. Burghardt, S.J., ed., *Women: New Dimensions* (New York: Paulist Press, 1975), p. 59.

are not innate drives, only culturally assigned roles which can—and should—be overcome.

Feminists note that men have been taught to exercise intellect, reason, courage, action, and initiative, while women have been taught to be weak, emotional, receptive, passive, and intuitive. However, they urge, both women and men should be all these things—strong and merciful, forceful and lenient, capable of intellect and intuition. Women and men should be wholly human: "androgynous" is the term some feminists use for such a state.[2]

Feminized-Christians have quickly picked up on these modern tendencies and have begun to apply them within their Christian communities, asserting that such beliefs are harmonious with Christian doctrine. Certain that God intended sexual differences to be overcome, they envision the eschatological age to come in which the Holy Spirit will be poured out and humanity will be changed, so that there no longer will be "male or female," as St Paul wrote (Gal 3.28).

The idea that men and women should be "androgynous" has been readily accepted by feminized-Christians who have begun to proclaim heaven to be a place full of "persons," neither male or female:

> . . . through holiness and ecstasy a woman transcends "nature" and participates in the eschatological sphere. She anticipates the order of salvation of heaven. In this eschatological order, sexual hierarchy is abolished for that asexual personhood in which there is "neither male or female."[3]

Feminized-Christians await such an eternal existence, and say further that those who experience the Holy Spirit on earth receive intimations of such a heaven.[4]

---

[2]Ibid., see pp. 158ff for a critique of this tenet widely accepted by feminists; also, Daly, *Beyond God the Father*, p. 15 and passim.

[3]Ruether and McLaughlin, *Women of Spirit*, p. 23.

[4]Eleanor McLaughlin, "The Christian Past: Does It Hold a Future for Women?" *Womanspirit Rising*, pp. 93–106.

More importantly, feminist theologians apply these anthropological theories to Jesus Christ. Jesus, they say, encompassed within Himself both masculine and feminine qualities: He was both strong and compassionate, both authoritative and meek. He fit no "machismo" image but rather combined within Himself the best of all human traits. He broke through the cultural, stereotypical roles placed upon women and men of His time (Jn 4.1–30). Being neither one-sidedly masculine nor feminine, He has been dubbed by feminized-Christians as the perfect androgyne, the perfect, whole human being.[5]

In addition feminized-Christians view the male body of Jesus as irrelevant and liken it in significance to the color of His eyes or His Jewish heritage. They consider His male body "temporary baggage" necessary only for His work on earth as a first-century male within a patriarchal culture and religion. If Christ had been incarnate as a woman in the first century, they reason, no one would have listened to Him; therefore, He chose to be incarnate as a male for the sole purpose of spreading His gospel message.[6] They view Him as gender-neutral and temporarily-sexed, for they believe He rose as a spiritual being into the heaven of asexuality. One feminist theologian writes:

> As a living human being Christ was a man. His sex was part of him: yet it was not his wholeness, and when he died he was freed from its limitations.[7]

---

[5]Una Kroll, *Flesh of My Flesh* (London: Darton, Longman & Todd, 1975), p. 100.

[6]Ruth Tiffany Barnhouse, "An Explanation of the Ordination of Women to the Priesthood in Terms of the Symbolism of the Eucharist," in *Women and Order*, ed. Robert L. Heyer (New York: Paulist Press, 1974), pp. 23–24.

[7]Kroll, *Flesh of My Flesh*, pp. 102–3.

Human Complementarity

What could an Orthodox Christian say about these tenets in general, and as applied to Jesus Christ in particular? Obviously both the Bible and Orthodox Christian hagiography support images of women and men as wholly human: they have the same human nature; they experience the same human emotions; they possess the same human virtues. A woman can be courageous: consider the female martyrs. A man can be weak: remember the Apostle Peter at the trial of Christ. Men and women equally partake in salvation and both are able to exhibit the fruits of the Holy Spirit (Gal 5.22–23) and the gifts of the Holy Spirit (1 Cor. 12); no prejudice toward either male or female exists.

However, a common human nature does not necessarily erase sex or gender distinction. Many strands of Orthodox Christian dogma refute the feminized-Christian extreme view that biology alone differentiates between women and men and that distinctions between the male and female sexes will be destroyed at death. Orthodox teaching suggests that masculinity and femininity are gifts from God to be used in personal expression; they are not cultural impositions.[8] Jesus Christ did not come to destroy (or overcome) the natural, God-willed distinction between the sexes, which He created for perfect goodness and order.

Genesis 2.18 states: "Then the Lord God said, 'It is not good that man should be alone, I will make him a helper fit for him.'" The word "helper" in this passage has a special meaning, deeper than the mundane rendering. "Helper" has as its Hebrew root *eser kenegdo*, the meaning of which Joan Schaupp explains in her book, *Woman, Image of the Holy Spirit*:

[8]". . . manhood and womanhood give to human nature a different form of existence both spiritually and bodily. It is proper to consider these differences to be relational and functional but at the same time innate." A quote from Professor Sergius Verhovskoy, "The Orthodox Understanding of the Relationship Between Man and Woman in the Christian Family," an unpublished article. Professor Verhovskoy was one of this author's teachers of Dogmatic Theology at St Vladimir's Seminary.

Vis-à-vis, the French term meaning face-to-face, is the expression used to capture the meaning of the Hebrew phrase, *eser kenegdo* ... Vis-à-vis would also have the connotation: counterpart, a mirror, a person created to help man discover himself. Scripture implies, therefore, that the woman is not a passive or inferior force, but the other half necessary for a mutually enriching dialogue ... real face-to-face discourse, meaningful contact with women, is probably necessary for man to achieve an integrated personality. *Eser kenegdo* implies this. For a balanced viewpoint, a male needs women friends, women co-workers, women associates in whatever his endeavor happens to be. Similarly women need male associates to develop integrated personalities.[9]

Certainly, this passage implies women and men were created to complement each other psychically, not just physically. Everything else in the garden was "good," but it was "not good" that Adam should be alone, therefore Eve was created to perfect the creation of humanity (Gen 2.18). God created not another male, and not just a female for procreation,[10] but a person whose body and feminine "mode of existence"—or "way of being human"—would complement the male biologically and his masculine mode psychologically. Humanity is expressed in two forms, equal but distinctive.

Jesus Christ, the Human Being

If Jesus Christ was truly incarnate as a human being, then He had to be of one sex and one gender,[11] either male or female, either

[9](Denville, NJ: Dimension Books, 1975), pp. 72–73.

[10]Many writings from the patristic tradition of the Orthodox Church in fact state that God created male and female forms of humanity in prevision of the fall, for the purpose of procreation. However, these writings represent only one side of a complex issue: see John Meyendorff, *Christ in Eastern Christian Thought* (Crestwood, NY: St Vladimir's Seminary Press, 1975), p. 232 n. 28.

[11]Jesus had no "sexual life" according to Orthodox Christian tradition, but He

masculine or feminine. But feminized-Christians are afraid that
such a supposition alienates women from the Lord completely. So,
they extend a theological argument: unless Jesus was somehow both
female and male, He could not have saved all of humanity. If He took
upon Himself just "maleness" only males could be saved. He had to
take on "humanness."[12]

This argument, seemingly straightforward, contains subtle flaws
because of conceptual imprecision. It deserves further examination
and elucidation.

The Orthodox Church too proclaims that Jesus Christ took on
human nature, but, a human nature *common* to women and men.
There are not "two human natures," male and female, but only one.
Jesus was the image of all humanity (Jn 19.5), and He took to Himself
the human nature that is the same for women and men (Phil 2.7).[13]

Nevertheless, human beings come in two forms, either male or
female. To be perfectly human, Jesus had to be incarnate in *one* of
these two forms. In short, the human nature Jesus had was common to both women and men but His particular sex was male and
His particular mode of existence was masculine. His "maleness"
was not a barrier to saving women, for His human nature—not His
maleness—was instrumental in His saving acts.[14] One cannot—and
need not—claim that He was both male and female, the "Divine
Androgyne."

Perhaps Jesus did not fit the masculine image as defined by
North American culture. He was compassionate, merciful, meek,
and motherly (Lk 13.34–35), but Scripture still *overwhelmingly* por-

was a male, and "masculine" in His relationship to the Church, His Bride. Feminists
have at times regarded the celibate life (virginal) as "asexual"—beyond sex and gender
distinctions. However, within Orthodox tradition, a virginal (or "angelic") existence
indicates a life (even and especially bodily life) ruled by the Spirit of God; it does not
connote asexuality.

[12]Wilkes, "Equal Rights on the Altar of God," pp. 106–8.

[13]Meyendorff, *Christ in Eastern Thought*, p. 74; see also the letter of St Cyril of
Alexandria to John of Antioch in NPNF, vol. 14, p. 251; cf. the *horos* of the Fourth
Ecumenical Council in that same volume.

[14]Ibid.

trays Him through male images and defines Him as masculine in His relationships. He is the Bridegroom (Jn 3.28–30), King (Lk 19.38), sacrificed Lamb (Rev 5.12), Servant of the Church (Lk 22.27), Head (Eph 5.21–32), and Savior (Eph 5.21–32). He is not the Bride, Queen, Body, or Handmaid. He is the New Adam and not the New Eve. He was not a stereotypical male, but He certainly was masculine. He was distinct, although not alienated, from woman. To know perfect masculinity, one may contemplate Jesus Christ; to know perfect femininity, one may contemplate His mother Mary.[15]

To further challenge the feminized-Christian viewpoint, one might ask: Was Jesus Christ merely the "spirit of humanity" entrapped in a male body or did He truly take on a human form? Are we ourselves merely human spirits trapped in male or female bodies or is biological sex integral to our human being? Was Jesus Christ like us or was He not?

If Jesus Christ was not incarnate as fully human, He could not have saved the human race. If He was not like us—either male or female—He could not have saved us. According to Orthodox Christian tradition, our Lord clothed Himself in our common humanity, in a male form, which (more startling to feminized-Christians) He keeps forever. Further, He continues to bear His masculine relationship to the Church, as Head, Lord, Savior, and Husband.

Beliefs about human nature impinge upon our beliefs about Jesus Christ. Obliterating or blurring sexual distinction in humanity leads to an androgynous Jesus. An androgynous Jesus does, of course, buttress the argument for a female priesthood: if the Lord embodies male and female, His priesthood would be complete only if women were included.[16] Therefore an Orthodox position that Jesus Christ possessed human nature in the male form becomes critical to the discussion of a female priesthood.

---

[15]The Virgin Mary, in Orthodox Christian tradition, is called the *Theotokos,* or Birth-giver of God, or Mother of God, and often is called "the Bride of God."

[16]Bozarth-Campbell, *Womanpriest,* p. 168.

The sex and gender of Jesus Christ is touched upon but not emphasized in Orthodox theology,[17] perhaps because the question is new to this era and was not of consequence to the Church in times past. Earlier theologians focused on the common humanity of Jesus Christ because it was an issue of their time. They were dealing with heresies that portrayed Jesus as superhuman, subhuman, or merely human. It was their task to declare Jesus Christ as consubstantial with women and men in their humanity and with God in His divinity.

However, new questions about humanity have been raised in this era. Nowadays the Church must begin to explore sexuality, femininity, and masculinity and to define the lines between heresy and Orthodoxy as new human models are applied to Jesus Christ.

By accepting an androgynous model for humanity, feminized-Christians have created an Androgynous Christ. They also have opened wide the door for justification of a female priesthood, by denying any significance between the sex and/or gender of the one great High Priest and His priesthood.[18] The problem is, a de-sexed Jesus Christ cannot save, for He is not fully human; and an ungendered Jesus Christ never did, and still does not, exist.

---

[17]St Gregory of Nazianzus, "Second Oration on Easter," NPNF, vol. 7, pp. 422–34; see especially paragraph XIII, p. 427. Also, St Theodore the Studite as quoted by Meyendorff in *Christ in Eastern Thought,* p. 186: "An indescribable Christ would also be an incorporeal Christ; but Isaiah (8.3) describes him as a male being (ἄρσην τεχθείς)."

[18]Issues of sex and gender have become complex. Some feminized-Christians indeed admit that women and men exercise peculiarly masculine and feminine spiritual gifts, but they claim that these complementary gifts only serve to enhance ministry within an inclusive priesthood.

CHAPTER 4

Feminism and the Resurrection

The belief in a bodily resurrection is another area of disagreement between feminized-Christians and traditional Orthodox Christians. As seen from the preceding section, feminized-Christians envision Jesus Christ, like all human beings, as being bound to a body only until His resurrection. After His resurrection, they claim, He was freed from His body—and male sex—and rose as an androgynous spirit. Feminized-Christians believe that the male body of Jesus was only "temporary." They deny that when Jesus rose from the dead He retained His identity as a male.

Likewise, feminist theologians assume that in the General Resurrection sexual differentiation will be abolished. People will be freed from their bodies and will rise as asexual persons. Then women will at last overcome the biological obstacle that had doomed them to be victims of oppression for so many centuries.

These are serious claims that stand in total opposition to Scripture (as interpreted at least by the Orthodox Christian Church), which clearly teaches there is a *bodily* resurrection. St Paul writes that after the physical body dies, there is another body, a spiritual body, a body transfigured. We will not be *disincarnate* but rather further clothed in immortality (2 Cor 5.2–4).

From the Orthodox point of view, humanity is restored to wholeness in the bodily resurrection.[1] Orthodox Christians cannot admit to or hope for a spiritual state that supports a dualistic existence—the opposition of soul to body, or the separation of soul and body. Feminist theologians propose broken beings, no longer

[1]Florovsky, *Creation*, p. 115.

49

human. To retain a body-soul correlation, even into the heavenly realm, remains crucial in Orthodox teaching.

St Irenaeus in the second century acknowledged that a perfect human being consisted of soul and body, vivified by the Spirit of God.[2] He further said that the body as well as the soul is made in the image of God. St Gregory of Nyssa likewise maintained that the soul is intimately connected to the body: the soul is the inward image of the body.[3]

Athenagoras of Athens specifically pointed out the importance of a bodily resurrection, saying, "Consequently, man must forever remain composed of soul and body. For if there is no resurrection, human nature is no longer human."[4] St Paul admonished the Church in Thessalonica: "May the God of peace Himself sanctify you wholly; and may your spirit and soul and body be kept sound and blameless at the coming of our Lord Jesus Christ" (1 Thess 5.23). Having a *body* is an essential part of being human.

The aforementioned Georges Florovsky noted:

> . . . mysterious as the union of soul and body indeed is, the immediate consciousness of man witnesses to the organic wholeness of his psycho-physical structure. This organic wholeness was from the very beginning strongly emphasized by all Christian teachers. That is why the separation of soul and body is the death of man himself, the discontinuation of his existence, of his wholeness . . . consequently, death and corruption of the body are sort of the fading away of the "image of God" in man.[5]

[2]A. Cleveland Cox, D.D., ed., *The Apostolic Fathers: Justin Martyr and Irenaeus* (Buffalo, NY: The Christian Literature Publishing Co., 1885), p. 531. Quoted from *Adv. Haer.* v. 6.

[3]Florovsky, *Creation*, p. 293, n. 6.

[4]Ibid., as quoted from *De resurrectione mort.*, p. 13. Written in the middle of the second century, this was the first theological essay on the Resurrection. In this same passage, the ancient author writes: ". . . soul and body compose in man one living entity."

[5]Ibid., p. 106.

Feminized-Christians generally downplay or deny any significant connection (or union) between soul and body.[6] It seems that the "union" and "unity" between soul and body expressed in the writings of the church fathers is absent from feminist theology. But, the significance of this "organic wholeness" (as Florovsky states) can best be found in the Orthodox Christian dogma regarding the resurrection of Jesus Christ.

Jesus: "Author and Finisher of Our Faith"

The Orthodox Christian viewpoint about the General Resurrection stems, naturally, from the Church's teaching on the resurrection of Jesus Christ Himself, whom Scripture calls the ". . . author and finisher of our faith, who for the joy that was set before him endured the Cross, despising its shame, and is set down at the right hand of the throne of God" (Heb 12.12). Denial of a bodily resurrection opposes the thought of St Paul:

> . . . if Christ has not been raised, then our preaching is in vain
> . . . If Christ has not been raised, your faith is futile and you
> are still in your sins (1 Cor 15.14, 17).

Scripture in no wise indicates that Jesus Christ shed His body in the resurrection. "The resurrection is called ἀνάστασις (*anastasis*); it is produced by a divine action indicated by the verb ἐγείρω (*egeiro*, to rouse from sleep). He who rises up, He who is woken up, is the same as He who lies down in the sleep of death."[7] Indeed, the point of the resurrection is that Jesus Christ *retained* His body—now incorrupt.

---

[6]Bozarth-Campbell, *Womanpriest*, p. 168. According to feminized-Christians, people can be a "little masculine" or a "little feminine," and their "personhood" is unrelated to their biological body. Feminist theologian Una Kroll stated: ". . . individuals have to work out for themselves the relationship that their anatomical sex has to their sexual orientation and self-perception." In *Flesh of My Flesh,* p. 91.

[7]F. X. Durwell, *The Resurrection* (New York: Sheed and Ward, 1960), p. 101.

And, following the "Author" and "Finisher" of our faith, we shall do the same in the General Resurrection.

Most of the New Testament attests to the fact that the resurrection from the dead is not release from the body but a new type of body (1 Cor 15.44). As F. X. Durwell noted in his work, *The Resurrection*:

> We have found in our text *nothing that denies the materiality of the body of the risen Christ*, but a confirmation of 1 Corinthians 15.45: "The New Adam was made into a quickening spirit."
>
> For in the Resurrection man will no longer be earthly, no longer nourished by the earth. Rooted in Christ, he will be nourished by the Spirit.[8]

Our bodies will be changed, quickened and nourished by the Spirit, our bodies will be incorrupt, and our bodies will remain. We will be raised as males and females, with "all our parts," so to speak. This idea, which scandalized the Greek mind long ago, may play havoc with the modern mind today; nevertheless it the teaching of the Orthodox Church. It is the hope of Orthodox Christians, their joy proclaimed on the Great Feast of Pascha:

> He who saved the three young men in the furnace became incarnate and suffered as a mortal man. Through His sufferings He clothed what is mortal in the robe of immortality. He alone is blessed and most glorious . . .[9]

---

[8]Ibid., p. 103.

[9]Ode 7 from the Canon of the Paschal (Easter) service of the Orthodox Christian Church. Some scriptural passages semingly concur with the feminist viewpoint when taken singly—Mk 16.12, 2 Pet 13–14, 2 Cor 5.8—but not when compared to other scriptural passages as interpreted within the tradition of the Church (2 Cor 5.2–5 and Lk 24.39).

To deny the bodily resurrection of Jesus Christ and to deny the bodily resurrection of Christians destroys the core of the Christian faith.

Feminized-Christians, through their denial of the bodily resurrection, have tried to make Jesus more palatable to women. If He is no longer male, then feminists could feel more comfortable as Christians; they could celebrate their "personhood" in a dead "Jesus" but an alive "Christ." They could also justify an argument for the female priesthood: if the risen Christ is no longer male, then women as well as men can bear His sacramental priesthood.

However, from the Orthodox Christian point of view, if Christ has not been raised, then our nature has not been saved; our bodies have not been restored; and we are still dead in our sins. Disincarnate in death, we lose the beauty and integrity and humanity God intended for us. We become shades of Sheol. The Good News is that God's plan for salvation integrates our souls and our bodies, by and through His resurrection.

Conclusion

The Women's Movement has presented opportunities to the Orthodox Church that she must not bypass. In every age in which doctrinal controversy has arisen the Orthodox Church has stood ready for debate. The Church must do the same in this age, in the midst of a religiously pluralistic society and in the presence of feminism. The subject of women in Christian communities has been brought to the fore, and the time has come to face all the issues it presents.

In view of the raging debate over the place of women and role of women in the Church, the Orthodox Church should examine policies toward her own female members. Questions about women being able to read and sing in church, women covering their heads during services,[1] and women partaking of the Eucharist during their menstrual cycles have not been settled in many Orthodox parishes. Now is the opportune time to review those policies and to see which ones preserve custom rather than tradition passed down by the Holy Spirit.

For example, in regard to receiving communion while menstruating, the Church must examine early Christian documents such as the *Didascalia Apostolorum*.[2]

---

[1]Veselin Kesich explains the dictate of St Paul in 1 Cor 11.2–16 in "St Paul: Anti-Feminist or Liberator?" *St Vladimir's Theological Quarterly* 21:3 (1977), pp. 135ff.

[2]The *Didascalia Apostolorum* ("The Teachings of the Apostles") is a document of the early Church, referred to in a publication of the Department of Education of the Greek Orthodox Archdiocese of America as a "work of respectable antiquity going back to the first half of the 3rd century" in *A Dictionary of Greek Orthodoxy,* by Rev. Nicon D. Patrinacos (1984). The *Didascalia* comprised the first section of the *Apostolic Constitutions,* which was rejected by the Synod in Trullo in AD 692, except for the 85 Apostolic Canons comprising the Appendix of the compilation. Strangely, the 85 Apostolic Canons themselves contain certain peculiarities: the 85th canon, in which the canonical books of the Old Testament and New Testament are enumerated, omits the Apocalypse of John but includes the *Apostolic Constitutions*!

For if thou think, O woman, that in the seven days of thy flux thou art void of the Holy Spirit; if thou die in those days, thou wilt depart empty and without hope. But if the Holy Spirit is always in thee, without just impediment dost thou keep thyself from prayer and from the Scriptures and from the Eucharist? . . . For if the Holy Spirit is in thee, why dost thou keep thyself from approaching to the works of the Holy Spirit? . . . Wherefore, beloved, flee and avoid such observances: for you have received release, that you should no more bind yourselves; and do not load yourselves again with that which our Lord and Savior has lifted from you. And do not observe these things, nor think them uncleanness; and do not refrain yourselves on their account, nor seek after sprinklings, or baptisms, or purification for these things.[3]

It is clear that in early times, Christian women were freed from the burdens of purification contained in the Jewish Law. Yet later these customs were revived, and even became part of a canonical letter[4] in the Church.[5]

In the fourth century, in his homily on Titus, St John Chrysostom reiterates the same position, stating it is only "sin" that can make

[3]*Didascalia Apostolorum,* the Syriac version, translated and accompanied by the Verona Latin fragments, with introduction and notes by R. Hugh Connolly (Oxford: Clarendon Press, 1929), pp. 244ff.

[4]The Letter of Blessed Dionysius, the Archbishop of Alexandria, to Basiledes the Bishop; listed as Canonical Letter II, in NPNF, vol. 14, p. 600 of the Appendix. This private letter was accepted into the body of canons of the Orthodox Church in Canon II of the Synod of Trullo (Quinisext Council), AD 692. The letter reads, in part: "Menstrous women ought not to come to the Holy Table, or touch the Holy of Holies, nor to the churches, but to pray elsewhere."

[5]The opinion of one bishop on a particular question does not have the same status as a canon in the Orthodox Church. St Photius of Constantinople states: "Everybody must preserve what was defined by ecumenical councils, but a particular opinion of a church father, or a definition issued by a local council can be followed by some and ignored by others." This was quoted by the Very Rev. John Meyendorff in *The Orthodox Church,* vol. 18.6, June 1982, p. 4, in an answer to a Letter to the Editor. However, it must be noted that the Letter of Blessed Dionysius has been accepted as a *canonical letter* by the Orthodox Church; see n. 4.

a person unclean before the Lord. The Jewish regulations regarding purification as described in the Book of Leviticus in the Old Testament were meant to be guidelines for righteous living. Therefore, said St John, if a person was made "unrighteous" by having natural emissions, how much more unrighteous would a person be by sinful actions of the mind and heart?[6] He never implies that Jewish purification rites should become an essential part of Christian communities; these prohibitions in the law were simply pedagogical, until the coming of Christ.

Another misconception prevalent in Orthodox communities is that laywomen are forbidden to enter the sanctuary but laymen may roam about that area at will. This notion directly contradicts historical fact.

Canon XLIV of the Synod of Laodicea (AD 343–381) does forbid women to enter the altar: "The altar must not be approached by women."[7] However, the reasons for this canon are not clear. One commentator advises that "insolent women" were overstepping the bounds of church order and rank and therefore were ousted from the sanctuary.[8] Another states that the menstrual cycle made women unworthy to approach.[9] Other evidence indicates that women were wandering about the altar area without a sense of propriety or were insisting on performing the offering, which was a function of the priest alone; therefore the clergy decided to exclude them from the sanctuary.[10] From this canon has come the notion that women—simply because they are of the female sex—are unworthy to enter the sanctuary.

This distorted conclusion does not take account of the canons as a whole. In fact, when studied *in toto*, the canons designate the altar as the domain of the *clergy*, to be kept free from confusion, disorder, and

[6]NPNF, vol. 13, pp. 528–31.
[7]NPNF, vol. 14, p. 153.
[8]Ibid.
[9]Ibid.
[10]This possibility is described by commentators on Canon XI of the Synod of Laodicea in NPNF, vol. 14, p. 130.

impiety. Any person not having liturgical business within the sanctuary should be excluded. Church canons forbid any layperson—male or female—from entering the sanctuary without the permission of the priest. Additionally, a layperson may not enter unless he or she has specific business to accomplish in the sanctuary.[11]

We have specific examples in the history of the Orthodox Church of women entering the altar area—even one in which a woman lays hold of the altar table itself! St Gregory of Nazianzus praised the piety of his sister Gorgonia when she fled to the altar to be healed of a malignant disease. He describes her as going to the sanctuary in the silence of the night, and crying and resting her head upon the altar, ". . . declaring that she would not loose her hold until she was made whole . . ."—and she was cured by the Lord![12] Deaconesses in the early Church were known to enter the sanctuary and to partake of Holy Communion from the chalice with the rest of the clergy.[13]

Even in today's monasteries, nuns serving as sacristans or candle bearers often enter the sanctuary; there are no men to serve in that capacity. A Carpatho-Russian liturgical tradition, prescribed in the marriage rite, requires the couple being wed to encircle the main altar in the sanctuary of the church during the ceremony; the couple typically encircles only the *analogion* (outer table in the church nave) in the marriage rite of other Orthodox Christian ethnic or national churches.

To consider an altar defiled because a woman has touched or approached it is a deviation from Orthodox thought. A woman able to receive the Eucharist certainly is able to enter the sanctuary where it has been prepared, since the Spirit of God sanctifies both men and women equally.

I am not advocating female acolytes ("altar girls") or a sudden improper influx of women into the altar area as a "right." The altar

[11]Canon LXIX, Quinisext Council, AD 692, ibid., p. 396.

[12]"On His Sister Gorgonia," NPNF, vol. 7, pp. 238ff.

[13]Roger Gryson, *The Ministry of Women in the Early Church* (Collegeville, MN: Liturgical Press, 1976), p. 66. Gryson describes the order of widows, who he claims held a rank analogous to that of deaconesses.

area must remain decorous, and generally girls and women have no reason to be within that area. However, the notion that women by virtue of their sex are less pure or less holy than men and therefore cannot enter the sanctuary is heresy.

An Orthodox Bulwark

In this present age, the Orthodox Church could cultivate in the faithful an attitude that St Jerome had toward women. In a culture generally demeaning to women, he praised their spirituality and intellect. He wrote to his friends, Paula and her daughter Eustochium, to whom he dedicated several of his works:

> There are people who take offense at seeing your name at the beginning of my works. These people do not know that while Barak trembled, Deborah saved Israel; that Esther delivered from supreme peril the children of God. I passed over in silence Anna and Elizabeth and all other holy women of the Gospel, but humble stars compared with the luminary, Mary. Is it not to women that our Lord appeared after His resurrection? Yes and the men could then blush for not having sought what the women had found.[14]

We Orthodox have a rich legacy about women that informs us the female sex is an inheritor of the salvation and grace given to us through Jesus Christ and the Holy Spirit (Gal 3.29). Now is the opportune time to review the lives of those female saints who have been prophetesses (Acts 21.9), missionaries,[15] deaconesses,[16] mar-

[14]"Preface to Commentary on Zephaniah," *Patrologia Greca* 25:1337ff, quoted in Nancy Hardesty, *Great Women of Faith* (Nashville: Baker Book House, 1980), p. 18.

[15]A missionary par excellence was St Nina. *The Life of St Nina, Equal of the Apostles and Enlightener of Georgia* [with a service and her life included], (Jordanville, NY: Holy Trinity Russian Orthodox Monastery, 1977). See also: Valerie G. Zahirsky, "St Nina, Evangelizer of Georgia" in *Enlighteners of Ancient Kingdoms* (Syosset, NY: DRE-Orthodox Church in America, 1980).

[16]Gryson, *The Ministry of Women in the Early Church,* passim.

tyrs, ascetics, rulers,[17] and theologians.[18] Now is the time to regard them and learn about their contributions to the Church.

Notwithstanding, in the face of actual heresies wrought by feminist theologians, the Orthodox Church must stand firm. Feminized-Christians accept beliefs about Scripture, terms for God, anthropology, Christology, and the resurrection that are disparate with Orthodox Christian thought and doctrine. On the surface, feminist arguments may seem just and fair to Orthodox Christians, but on a deeper level, central doctrines are being pushed aside and replaced by humanistic ideals. The revelation of God is being replaced by human philosophy, and this is injurious not only to the Christian faith but also to humanity.

The Orthodox Church must stand as a corrective to both radically feminist *and* misogynistic ideals. The Church's tradition offers the true vision of the human community that God wills, and a true vision of God that humanity must embrace to be saved. The Church must continue to stand as a bulwark of truth, a light to the nations and a guide to the blind (Rom 2.19)—indeed, as it has done in every era.

[17]Hardesty, *Great Women of Faith*, pp. 21–26. Hardesty cites the life of St Pulcheria as an example. Cf. Stephen Bobulsky, "St Pulcheria" in *Rulers of Nations, Servants of Christ* (Syosset, NY: DRE-Orthodox Church in America, 1980); Jan Koczak and Mark Stokoe, *Women Martyrs of the Lord* (Syosset, NY: DRE-Orthodox Church in America, 1981).

[18]Some feast day hymns to female Orthodox saints attest to this. The hymn to St Euphemia (+304) (September 16 celebration) reads: "You have manifested reason . . . by the visitation of the Holy Spirit you instructed the assembly of the Holy Fathers." The hymn sung on the feast of Holy Hieromartyrs Dionysius and Cyprian (October 3) refers to the virgin Justina: "When Dionysius rejected the Stoic philosophers and became a disciple of the gnostics . . . then he was enlightened by the most beautiful virgin Justina . . . he fled the treachery of demons and after destroying the books of sorcery he became a herald of the Gospel." St Jerome records that the widow Marcella was the first in the Church to discover the heresies of Origen; she perceived them before the clergy or laymen of the Church ("Letter CXXVII to Principia from Jerome," NPNF, vol. 6, p. 256).

Acknowledgments

Credits are given to the following authors and publishers for excerpts, taken from—

Flesh of My Flesh, by Una Kroll, published and copyrighted 1975 by Darton, Longman and Todd, Ltd., London, and used by the permission of the publishers.

The Resurrection, by F. X. Durwell, published and copyrighted 1960 by Sheed and Ward, New York, and used by the permission of the publishers.

Womanpriest: A Personal Odyssey, by Alla Bozarth-Campbell, published and copyrighted 1978 by Paulist Press, New York, and used by the permission of the author.

Aspects of Church History: Volume Four in the Collected Works of Georges Florovsky, and *Creation and Redemption: Volume Three in the Collected Works of Georges Florovsky,* by Georges Florovsky, published and copyrighted 1975 by Nordland Publishing Company, Belmont, MA, and used by the permission of the publishers.

A Priest Forever, by Carter Heywood, copyrighted 1976 by Carter Heywood, published by Harper & Row, New York, and used by the permission of the publishers.

A Select Library of Nicene and Post-Nicene Fathers of the Christian Church, Volumes V and VII, Schaff, Philip, D.D., L.L.D., and Wace, Henry, D.D., eds., published and copyrighted 1892 by Wm. B. Eerdmans Publishing Company, Grand Rapids, Michigan, and used by the permission of the publishers.

It Changed My Life, by Betty Friedan, published and copyrighted 1963 by Random House, Inc., New York, and used by the permission of the publishers.

Woman: New Dimensions, by Walter J. Burghardt, S.J., ed., published and copyrighted 1975 by Paulist Press, New York, and used by the permission of the publishers.

Women and Order, by Robert J. Heyer, ed., published and copyrighted 1974 by Paulist Press, New York, and used by the permission of the publishers.

The Spirit of God, by Thomas Hopko, published and copyrighted 1976 by Morehouse-Barlow Co., Inc., Wilton, CT, and used by the permission of the publishers.

Asking the Fathers, by Aelred Squire, published and copyrighted 1973 by SPCK, London, and used by the permission of the publishers.

Christ in Eastern Christian Thought, by John Meyendorff, published and copyrighted 1975 by St Vladimir's Seminary Press, Crestwood, NY, and used by the permission of the publishers.

In the Image and Likeness of God, by Vladimir Lossky, published and copyrighted 1974 by St Vladimir's Seminary Press, Crestwood, NY, and used by the permission of the publishers.

Orthodox Theology: An Introduction, by Vladimir Lossky, published and copyrighted 1978 by St Vladimir's Seminary Press, Crestwood, NY, and used by the permission of the publishers.

Woman: Image of the Holy Spirit, by Joan Schaupp, published and copyrighted 1975 by Dimension Books, Denville, NJ, and used by the permission of the publishers.

Great Women of Faith, by Nancy Hardesty, copyrighted 1980 by Baker Book House, and used by permission of the publishers.

Appreciation is also extended by the author to Sister Elizabeth of the Community of the Holy Myrrhbearers for her editorial assistance with this work.

Select Bibliography

Bobulsky, Stephen. *Rulers of Nations, Servants of Christ.* "St Pulcheria." Syosset, NY: DRE-Orthodox Church in America, 1980.

Bouyer, Louis. *Women in the Church.* San Francisco: Ignatius Press, 1979.

Chrysostom, St John. "Epistle to Titus." Philip Schaff and Henry Wace, eds. *A Select Library of Nicene and Post-Nicene Fathers.* Grand Rapids, Michigan: Wm. B. Eerdmans Publishing Co., 1892. Vol. 13, second series. *Homilies on the Epistles of St Paul the Apostle to Timothy, Titus and Philemon.* Philip Schaff, tr.

Danielou, Jean. *The Ministry of Women in the Early Church.* Leighton Buzzard, Great Britain: The Faith Press, 1961.

Didascalia Apostolorum (the Syriac version). Translated and accompanied by the Verona Latin fragments with introduction and notes by R. Hugh Connolly. Oxford: Claredon Press, 1929.

Gryson, Roger. *The Ministry of Women in the Early Church.* Collegeville, MN: The Liturgical Press, 1976.

Hardesty, Nancy A. *Great Women of Faith.* Nashville: Abingdon Press, 1982.

Hopko, Thomas, ed. *Woman and the Priesthood.* Crestwood, NY: SVS Press, 1983.

_____. *Women and Men in the Church: A Study of the Community of Women and Men in the Church.* Syosset, NY: DRE-Orthodox Church in America, 1980.

Kesich, Veselin. "St Paul: Anti-Feminist or Liberator?," *St Vladimir's Theological Quarterly* 21:3 (1977): 123–147.

Koczak, Jan and Mark Stokoe. *Women Martyrs of the Lord.* Syosset, NY: DRE-Orthodox Church in America, 1981.

The Life of St Nina, Equal of the Apostles and Enlightener of Georgia. Jordanville, NY: Holy Trinity Russian Orthodox Monastery, 1977.

Luke, Helen M. *Woman Earth and Spirit: The Feminine in Symbol and Myth.* New York: Crossroads, 1981.

Nazianzen, St Gregory. "On His Sister Gorgonia." Philip Schaff and Henry
    Wace, eds. *A Select Library of Nicene and Post Nicene Fathers.* Grand
    Rapids, MI: Wm. B. Eerdmans Publishing Company, 1892. Vol. 7, second
    series. *Select Orations of St Gregory Nazianzen.* Charles Browne and
    James Swallow, trs.

The Northern Thebaid: Monastic Saints of the Russian North. Platina, CA: St
    Herman of Alaska Brotherhood, 1975.

Priklonsky, Alexander. *Blessed Athanasia: Disciple of St Seraphim.* Platina,
    CA: St Herman of Alaska Brotherhood, 1975.

The Principal Works of St Jerome. Philip Schaff and Henry Wace, eds. *A Select
    Library of Nicene and Post Nicene Fathers.* Grand Rapids, MI: Wm. B.
    Eerdmans Publishing Company, 1892. Vol. 6, second series, reprint ed.
    1979. W. H. Gremantle, tr.

Schaupp, Joan. *Woman: Image of the Holy Spirit.* Denville, NJ: Dimension
    Books, 1975.

Schmidt, Gail Ramshaw. "Lutheran Liturgical Prayer and God as Mother."
    Worship 52:6 (November 1978): 517–542.

Tournier, Paul. *The Gift of Feeling.* Atlanta: John Knox Press, 1981.

Zahirsky, Valerie G. "St Nina, Evangelizer of Georgia." *Enlighteners of
    Ancient Kingdoms.* Syosset, NY: DRE-Orthodox Church in America,
    1980.